PIANO SOLO

FIRST MAN

MUSIC FROM THE
MOTION PICTURE SOUNDTRACK

MUSIC BY JUSTIN HURWITZ

ISBN 978-1-5400-4363-4

Visit Hal Leonard Online at
www.halleonard.com

Contact Us:
Hal Leonard
7777 West Bluemound Road
Milwaukee, WI 53213
Email: info@halleonard.com

In Europe contact:
Hal Leonard Europe Limited
42 Wigmore Street
Marylebone, London, W1U 2RN
Email: info@halleonardeurope.com

In Australia contact:
Hal Leonard Australia Pty. Ltd.
4 Lentara Court
Cheltenham, Victoria, 3192 Australia
Email: info@halleonard.com.au

KAREN

By JUSTIN HURWITZ

Very slowly and freely

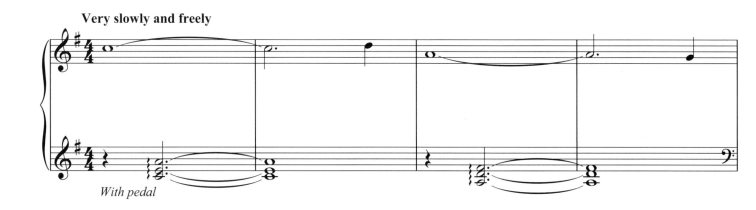

With pedal

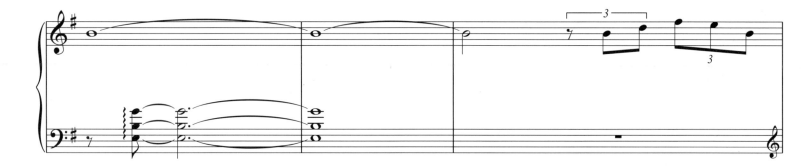

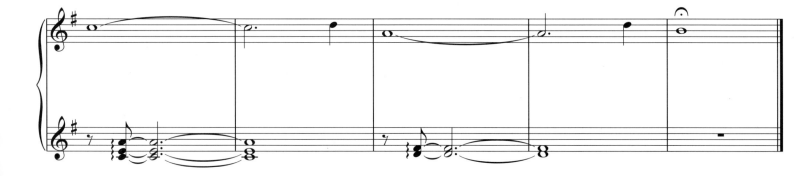

HOUSTON

By JUSTIN HURWITZ

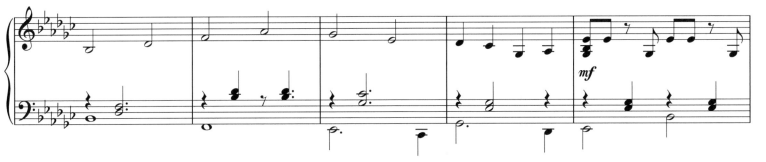

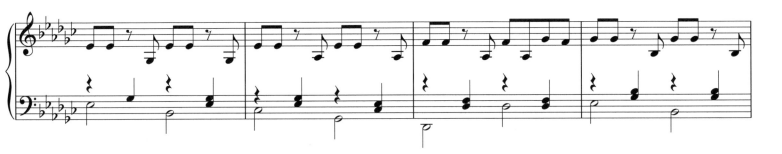

MULTI-AXIS TRAINER

By JUSTIN HURWITZ

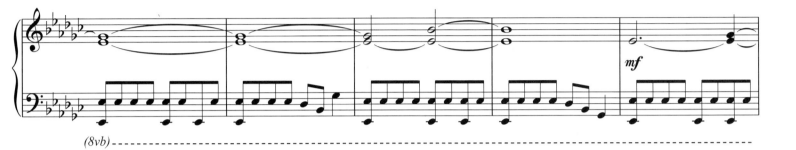

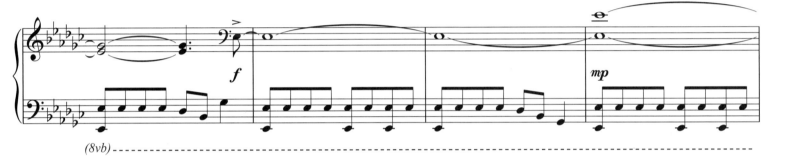

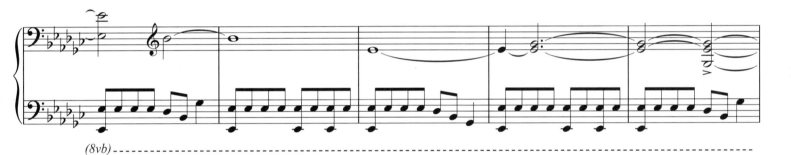

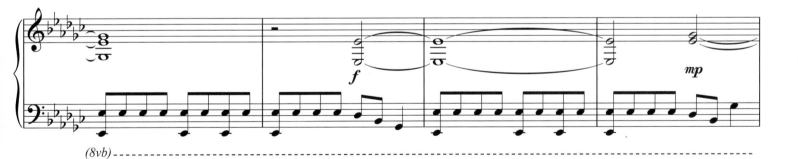

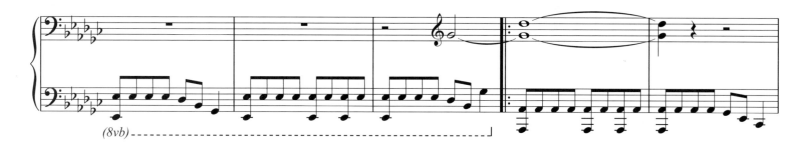

SQUAWK BOX

By JUSTIN HURWITZ

Very slowly, with freedom

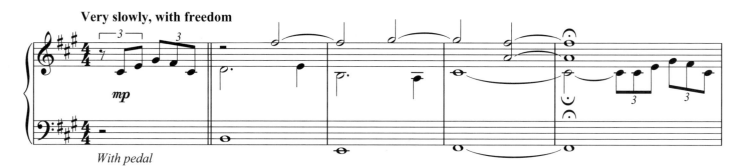

mp

With pedal

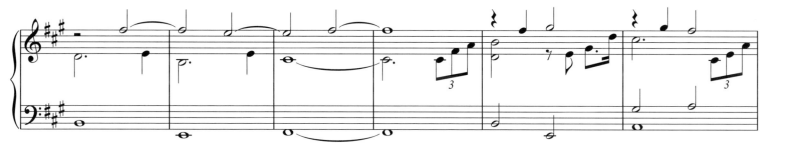

DOCKING WALTZ

By JUSTIN HURWITZ

Moderately

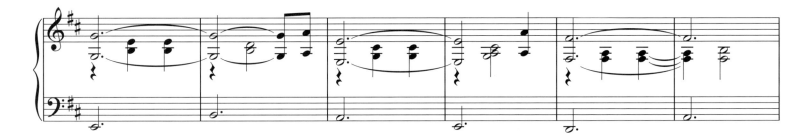

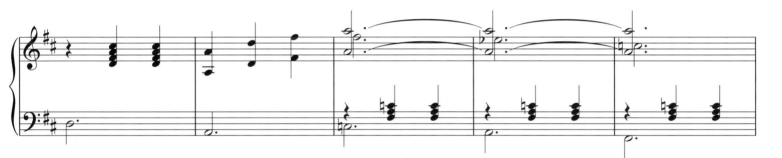

THE ARMSTRONGS

By JUSTIN HURWITZ

dim. poco a poco

poco rit.

pp

APOLLO 11 LAUNCH

By JUSTIN HURWITZ

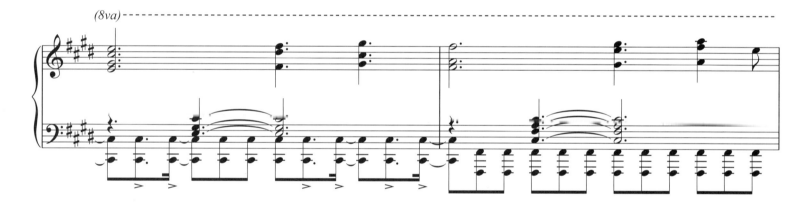

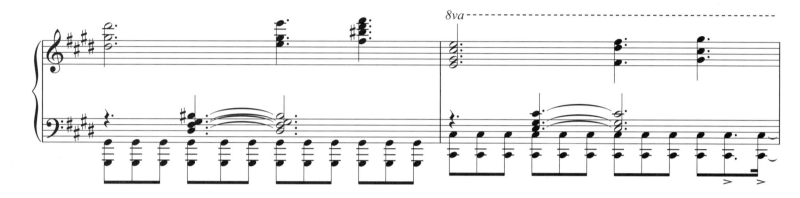

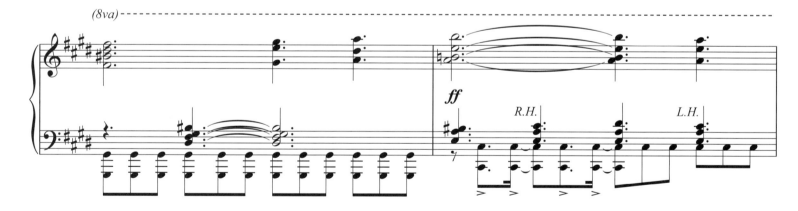

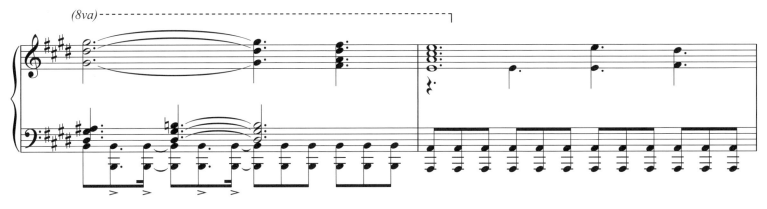

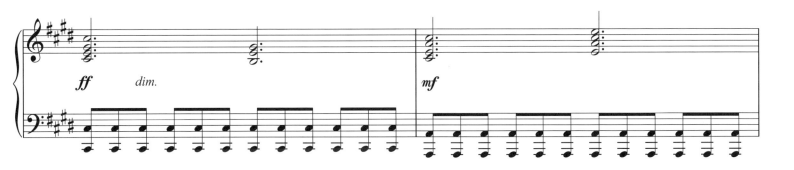

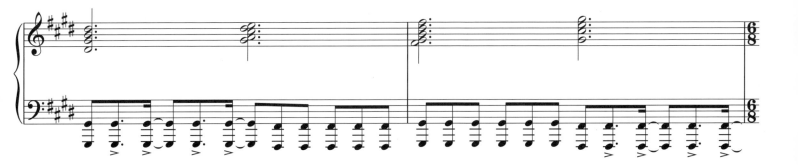

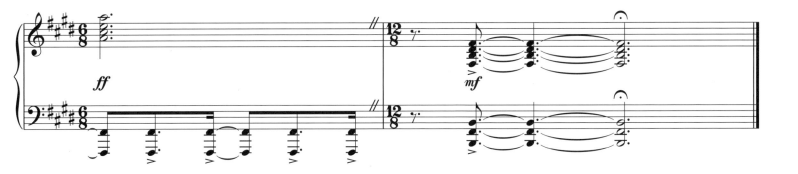

THE LANDING

By JUSTIN HURWITZ

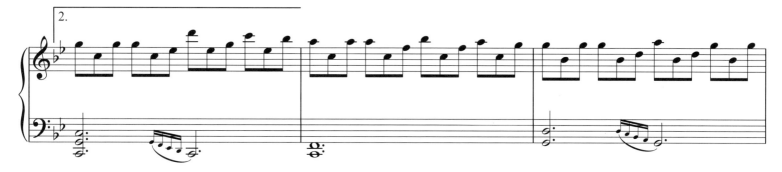

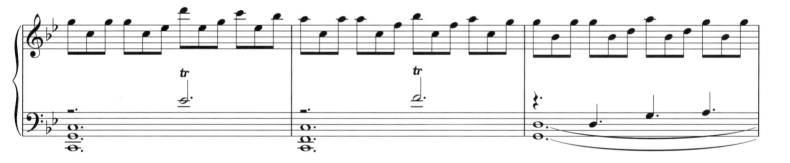

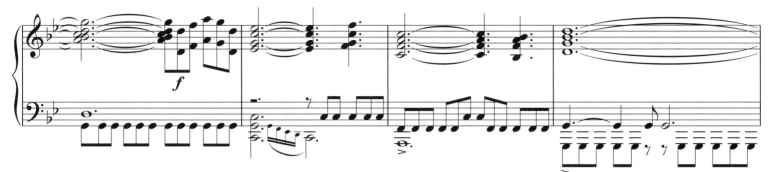

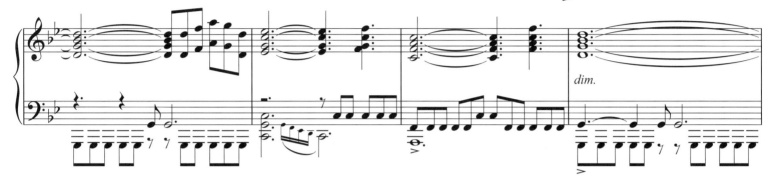

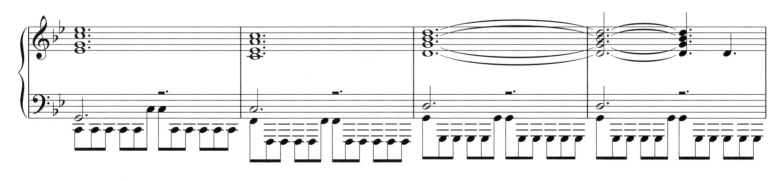

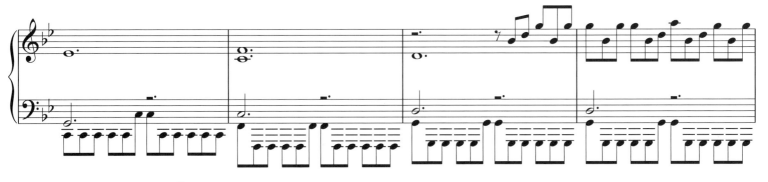

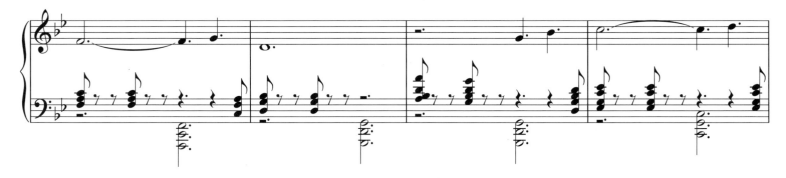

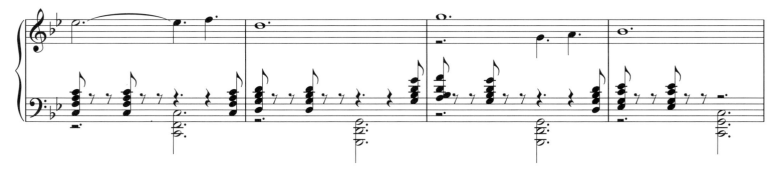

CRATER

By JUSTIN HURWITZ

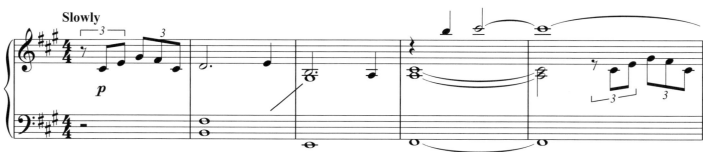

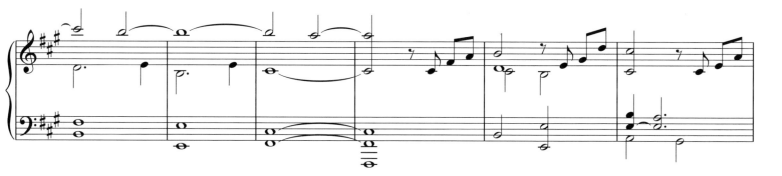

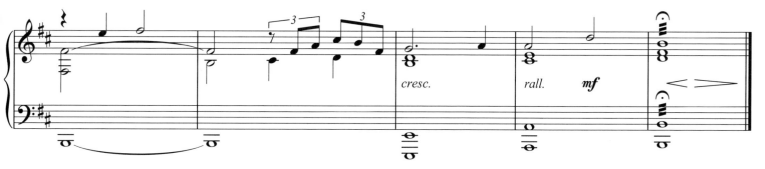

QUARANTINE

By JUSTIN HURWITZ

Moderately slow, expressively

Pedal ad lib. throughout

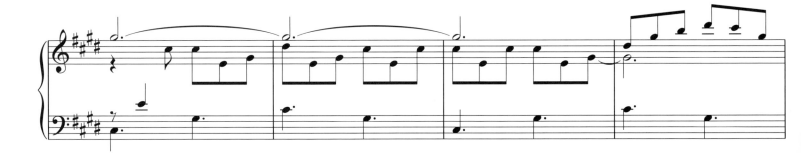

rit.　　　　*a tempo*

rit.

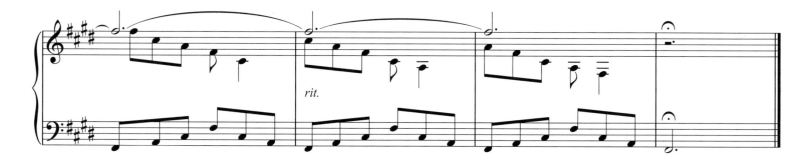

END CREDITS

By JUSTIN HURWITZ

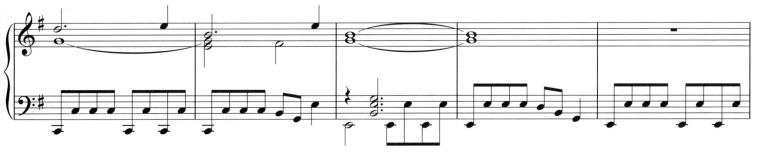

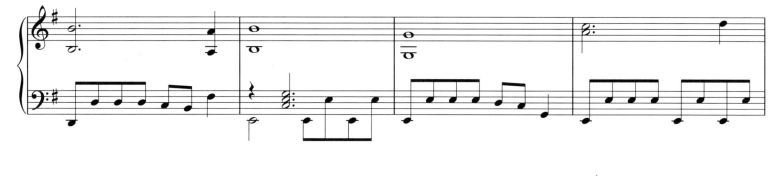

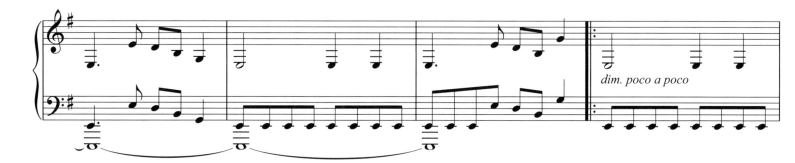

Play 5 times

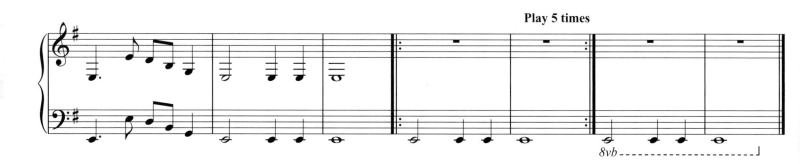

8vb - ┘